Affirmations on Demand:

1000 Affirmations to Change Your Mindset and Change Your Life

By

Jessica Leichtweisz
and
Dr. Aikyna Finch

How to Use This Book

Affirmations are a powerful way to quickly change your life by changing the way that you think about yourself. Working on our mindset is an every day and never ending process. It is often said that if we are not growing, we are dying. At Changing Minds Online, we believe in committing time daily to shifting our mindset to one of abundance.

One of the things that we have noticed in our practice is that every day as events play out in our lives, areas that require we shift to a more abundant become more and more apparent and those areas are always changing. One day, what seems like a strength can quickly and easily become an area of weakness.

But, what if just as easily, that area of weakness can become a strength? We believe it can and that's why we created this book. You can use this book to pinpoint specific areas of your mindset that require attention and reprogram them to abundant and rewarding beliefs. Simply, choose an area that requires attention, open the page to that section and read the affirmations out loud. Doing so literally and immediately will change your neurology. You will instantly begin to change your mindset and your vibrational energy will become a powerful attractor to whatever it is that you want.

Do this daily and watch as your life begins to change right before your eyes. You can be, do and have whatever you want IF your mindset is aligned with what you want. Using this book daily will ensure that you are aligned with your source of power and have the most abundant and powerful mindset possible.

Table of Contents

Abundance

I attract abundance with ease
I am abundant.
I love in an abundant world.
Great things are on their way
I can be, do and have anything I dream.
I deserve to manifest miracles.
I was created to live an abundant life.
I have everything that I require.
I am enough.
I live in abundant world.
I Believe...I Achieve...I Receive.
I live in a place of abundance.
My energy radiates abundance daily.
I grow in abundance everyday.
I know that abundance was meant for me.
I am blessed daily.
I feel abundance coming to me.
I claim all of the blessings in my life.
I move in the direction of my dreams.
I can do anything in my life.

Authenticity

I am authentic.
I am true to myself.
I deserve to follow my heart.
I love all parts of me, the good and the bad.
I am free to be myself.
I deserve to express myself authentically.
People love me for who I am.
It's okay to be me.
I let people see the real me.
I can be myself.
I am who I am for a reason.
I live in my truth.
I will always be true to myself.
I live a life I designed.
My self-awareness grows daily.
My dreams are tailored to me.
I share the true me with the world.
I feel the true me coming forward daily.
I can grow into the person I am meant to be.
I will let the real me shine through.

Beauty

I am beautiful.
I love myself.
I love who I see in the mirror.
I have a sexy body.
I have a gorgeous smile.
People find me attractive.
I find myself attractive.
I love myself completely.
I have a great body.
People find me beautiful.
There is beauty all around me.
I see the beauty in others.
I am beautiful by design.
I attract beauty.
I have beauty surrounding me.
I live a beautiful existence.
My beauty grows daily.
I am building a beautiful world.
I am my own kind of beautiful.
I love my beautiful life.

Belief

I believe in myself.
I believe I am successful.
I believe I can achieve my goals.
I believe in my ability to manifest miracles.
I believe in purpose.
I believe in self-respect.
I believe in truth.
My beliefs are my foundation.
My beliefs can change the world.
I believe that dreams are limitless.
I believe that I am worthy.
I believe I have all I need to be whole.
I believe I will move in my greatness.
My beliefs move me in the right direction.
My beliefs shape my future.
I believe that there is a purpose for everyone.
I believe that I am powerful.
I believe that life can be created by design.
I believe there is goodness in others.
I believe in love.

Blessing

I am blessed.
I am in God and God is in me.
I am created by the divine.
God lives in me.
I was created to live an abundant life.
God wants to bless me.
I am receiving blessings right now.
I was made in the image of God.
I am blessed beyond measure.
I have the ability to move mountains.
If I ask, I shall receive.
If I see, I shall find.
Blessings are flowing in my life.
I move in the direction of my blessings.
I feel the blessings moving my way.
I am blessed with abundance.
I am thankful for all of the blessings in my life.
I love to bless others.
I share my blessings with others.
Blessings are gifts from God.

Certainty

I have certainty, clarity and peace of mind.
I am certain I will succeed.
I am certain I have found my purpose.
I am certain I have what it takes.
I speak with certainty.
I speak with conviction and authority.
I am a natural born leader.
People trust me.
What I have to say matters.
I trust myself.
I am certain about my abilities.
I am certain in my thoughts.
I am certain good things will happen.
I am certain I will make things happen.
I am certain I will change lives.
I am certain I will step out on faith.
I am certain I will conquer my fears.
I am certain I will make my mark on the world.
I am certain I will live in my purpose.
I am certain I will meet my full potential.

Change

♥

I embrace change.
I am willing to step outside of my comfort zone.
My life is changing for the better.
Change excites me!
I am changing right now.
I will change and grow for the better
Change has led to higher heights.
I share the abundance that change brings.
I use change to reach new levels in my life.
Change stretches my comfort zone.
I feel change happening in my life.
I know that change is necessary.
I live in a place of change.
Change brings new beginnings.
I make change work for my good.
I have decided to go with the flow of change.
I love to see the changes in my life.
Change makes me grow.
I know change is a part of life.
I welcome change.

Clarity

I am clear on what my purpose is.
I have clarity, certainty and peace of mind.
I have a clear vision for my life.
I receive clarity from God when I ask for it.
I am clear about what I want.
I send clear signals to the universe.
I see my goals with clarity.
I have clarity in my mind.
It is wonderful I have clarity about my purpose in life.
I have a clear vision for executing my goals.
I am clear about my direction.
I am clear about my purpose.
I am clear about my focus.
I am clear about my journey in life.
I am clear about my thoughts.
I am clear about creating my life.
I see the goodness in the world.
I see the love all around me.
I am clear about my place in the world.
I see the joy around me.

Commitment

I am committed to what I start.
I am committed to my success.
I have committed and fulfilling relationships.
I am committed to myself.
I am committed to living in my purpose.
I am committed to upholding my values.
I finish what I start every time.
I close deals.
I am committed to my clients.
I am committed to the people I love.
I am committed to my goals.
I am committed to my happiness.
I am committed to changing the world.
I am committed to helping others.
I am committed to creating my life by design.
I am committed to moving to my next level.
I am committed to making my dreams come true.
I am committed to my mission.
I am committed to my faith.
I am committed to love.

Confidence

I am willing to step outside of my comfort zone.
I choose to approach others with confidence.
I have the knowledge and resources to achieve my dreams.
I am proud of myself.
I fully accept myself and know that I am worthy of great things in life.
I am secure.
I can manifest my dreams.
I will make my dreams come true.
I will live in my purpose.
Nothing will claim my power.
I know who I am.
I am confident in my journey to greatness.
I am confident in my purpose.
I am confident in my need to make an impact.
I will let others know they are enough.
I will share my confidence with other.
I am confident in my abilities.
I am confident in myself.
I will encourage everyone I meet.
I will give my best to the world.

Connection

I am never alone.
There are many people that love me and care about
me.
There are people who support me all around me.
People want me to be successful.
I attract people in my life that want to support me.
I hold others in possibility.
I see the good in others and others see the good in
me.
I feel connected to others.
I have excellent communication skills.
People get me.
I have a strong support system.
I build strong communities.
I attract great people in my life.
I am living the life of a connector.
I am growing great connections.
I am a part of a great support system.
I make real connections.
I will create a strong and supportive circle.
I love to move in supportive circles.
I am connected to powerful people.

Courage

I have the courage to change.
I have the courage to love myself.
I have the courage to take risks.
I am courageous.
I am bold.
I step outside of my comfort zone.
I stand up for what I believe in.
I am willing to take risks.
I am fearless.
I stand strong in courage and faith.
I have to stand in my truth.
I am living my life outside of fear.
I have the courage to live an awesome life.
I have the courage to do the right thing.
I am powerful.
I am moving my obstacles.
I have the courage to make things happen.
I have the courage to conquer my fears.
I am a powerful force.
I stand in my convictions.

Creativity

I am creative.
I am constantly coming up with new ideas.
People look to me to come up with a solution.
I am imaginative.
I channel creative energy.
I add value to projects and ideas.
I am innovative.
I can create my life.
I am designing my future.
People look to me for ideas and inspiration.
I believe in my creative skills.
I see innovation all around me.
I use innovation in all I do.
I feel creative daily.
Creativity is necessary.
I am attracted to creativity.
I design beautiful things.
I am full of ideas.
I see the creativity in the world.
I love to design.

Determination

I will win.
I finish what I start.
I am determined to succeed.
I never give up.
I am an unstoppable force.
I will see this through.
I am determined to achieve my goals,
I will be victorious.
Success is the only option.
I have determination and motivation.
Determination is necessary for success.
I believe in my determination.
I know my dreams will come true.
I am going for the goal daily.
I am moving in the right direction for greatness.
I am in control of my life.
I will let the world know who I am.
I am going to get what I want.
I am going to make it happen.
I am determined.

Employment

Everyone wants to hire me.
I have so much to contribute.
I am an asset to any company.
I will bring value to the next company I join.
I am a loyal employee.
I deserve a great job.
I deserve to be paid what I am worth.
I have a job I love.
I am excited to go to work every morning.
I bless others with my products and services.
I am expanding the community with my work.
I am worth my pay.
I am a rock star at work.
I grow in knowledge daily.
I share my work with others.
I help others with my work.
I am blessed to work in my purpose.
I love what I do.
I am valuable to my company.
I have a great skillset.

Energy

I live in my ideal body.
I can do anything that I want.
My energy attracts greatness.
My energy is filled with love.
I live my life with high energy.
I have the energy to get things done.
I make my energy to work for me.
I move with great energy.
I have the energy to make my dreams come true.
I attract people with positive energy.
I keep positive energy flowing.
I turn my negative energy to positive.
My energy changes lives.
I make the energy around me positive.
I will shift the energy for greatness.
I change the energy in the room.
I live in an environment of positive energy.
I feel the energy of others.
I move in positive energy.
I have magnetic energy.

Faith

Everything will work out.
I trust in myself.
I trust everything I need will be provided.
I am safe.
Everything happens for my good.
I believe in myself.
All things are possible.
Things are going to turn out amazing.
I stand in faith.
I am willing to take risks.
I am faithful.
I have strong faith.
My faith is my cornerstone.
I am living in my faith.
My faith grows daily.
I share my faith daily.
I have faithful relationships.
Faith is necessary.
Faith is part of success.
My faith is true.

Family

My family is my greatest blessing.
I put my family first.
My family loves me and understands me.
My family supports my dreams.
My family will always be there for me.
I am a blessing to my family.
I am a role model to my family.
My family's love will last forever.
I hold my family close to my heart.
I take time to nurture my relationships.
I love spending time with my family.
I love supporting my family.
I learn from my family.
I am who I am because of my family.
Family is a place of love.
I gain power from my family.
I have a strong relationship with my family.
I am in love with my family.
Family is necessary.
I am family oriented.

Forgiveness

I am forgiven.
I forgive others.
I forgive myself.
Forgiveness is necessary.
Forgiveness changes lives.
Forgiveness is a gift.
I chose to forgive others.
My sins are forgiven.
Forgiveness is free.
I make forgiveness a priority.
I will forgive.
Forgiveness is a game changer.
Forgiveness is powerful.
I will share forgiveness with others.
I will teach others about forgiveness.
Forgiveness should be given freely.
I forgive people who tried the take my power.
I forgive people who hurt me.
I forgive all past wrongs.
I forgive all past hurts.

Freedom

I am free.
I am free of bondage.
I am free of trials.
I am free of negativity.
I am free of fear.
I am free of the past.
Freedom changes lives.
I am taking my life back.
I am breaking the chains over my life.
Freedom is necessary.
I am free of heartache.
I am free of confusion.
I am free of stress.
I am free of pain.
I am free of worry.
I am debt free.
I am financially free.
I am free to be
I am free of struggle
I am free of limits

Friendship

People love me.
I have great friendships.
My friends can trust me and count on me.
I can trust and count on my friends.
I have meaningful relationships.
My friends care about me.
My friends want me to succeed.
I take time to cultivate relationships.
I value the people in my life closest to me.
I have loving relationships.
I have longtime friends
I have friends that understand me.
My friends love me for me.
My friends expose me to different things.
I like spending time with my friends.
Friends help you grow.
I am a supportive friend.
I love my friends.
I have a strong support system.
Friends are necessary.

Gratitude

I am blessed.
I am grateful for this amazing life I am living.
I am grateful for love.
I am full of gratitude.
I share gratitude with others.
I am grateful for grace.
I am grateful for mercy.
Gratitude changes lives.
I move in gratitude.
I am grateful for abundance.
I am grateful for positive energy.
I have an attitude of gratitude.
I know the power of gratitude in my life.
I am grateful for a strong support system.
I am grateful for who I am.
I show gratitude daily.
Gratitude is necessary.
I am grateful for family.
I am grateful for success.
I live in a state of gratitude.

Growth

I have learned from failure.
I am always growing.
I learn new things every day.
I have upward mobility.
I am always moving forward.
My business is expanding.
My love for others grows every day.
I am constantly developing my mindset.
I learn from others.
I am expanding in influence and power.
I am developing myself daily.
I love to educate others.
I see the growth all around me.
My life is expanding everyday.
My skills are expanding.
I will grow in all aspects of my life.
I am ready to expand myself.
I am moving in upward mobility.
I am living in my growth.
I am growing daily.

Happiness

I choose to be happy.
I am happy.
I choose my emotions.
I see the good in all situations.
I live in a state of happiness.
My happiness is unbreakable.
I radiate happiness.
I feel the happiness grow in me daily.
I am the happiest I have ever been.
I move in a state of happiness.
I crave happiness in my life.
Happiness is a way of life.
I see the power in happiness.
I am happy in all areas of my life.
I love being happy.
Happiness is necessary.
I deserve all the happiness in the world.
I love to share happiness with others.
I make others happy.
I will make happiness the norm.

Healing

I am healed.
My body is whole.
I am complete.
My body is made perfectly.
My body can heal itself.
My body knows what it needs.
I honor my body.
My body is made by the divine.
I can work miracles right now.
I am perfect.
I am healing my soul.
My spirit is whole.
I am looking for total healing.
I will be healed completely.
I am a healer.
I see the healing happening in my life.
I know I will be healed.
I have a powerful heart.
I live in a healing world.
I am healing my heart.

Health

I live in my ideal body.
I am full of energy.
I have a strong immune system.
My bones are healthy and strong.
I am fit and healthy.
I am healthy in mind and spirit.
I have clarity.
I sleep soundly.
I wake up ready to take on the world.
I honor my body.
I am full of spirit.
I am feeling healthy.
I am growing in strength.
My body is beautiful.
I am excited about being healthy.
I love to exercise.
I love the shape that I am in.
I treat my body like a temple.
I put healthy things in my body.
I am whole.

Honesty

I am truthful and honest.
I am honest with myself.
I value my integrity.
People trust me.
I am trusting of others.
I always do what I say.
My word is gold.
I trust my judgment.
I surround myself with honest people.
I always tell the truth.
I am leaving the mask behind.
My truth is real.
I feel when I can trust others.
I see the honesty in others.
I believe in my intuition.
My feelings are real.
I always let people know how I feel.
I am honest with others.
I am known for my realness.
I am true to myself.

Inspiration

I surround myself with people who inspire me.
I inspire others.
I am inspired.
I am in tune to the wisdom of the universe.
I always have upbeat energy that inspires.
People look up to me.
I have mentors to look up to.
The people I choose to spend my time with life me
up.
I take time for inspiration.
I inspire myself.
I believe in inspiration.
Inspiration surrounds me.
Inspiration is necessary.
Inspiration is a source of power.
My inspiration is everything to me.
People look to me for inspiration.
I am an inspiration.
I have an inspiration circle.
I inspire others to go after their dreams.
I inspire people to be great.

Integrity

I build up others with my words.
My actions reflect my values.
I have integrity.
I have values.
I move in the power of my values.
I attract others that live in integrity.
I encourage others to live in integrity.
My power comes from living in integrity.
I will choose the right path.
I will share my true story to inspire others.
I will tell the truth at all times.
I will honor my intuition.
I have to move towards honesty at all times.
My gifts work in integrity.
My purpose is built in integrity.
I will always stand in my beliefs.
I walk in truth.
I am who I say I am.
I live in my beliefs.
I am true to my beliefs and myself.

Joy

I choose to be joyful.
I am joyful.
I choose my emotions.
I see the good in all situations.
Joy is necessary.
Joy is powerful.
Joy is a game changer.
I share joy with others.
I live in a place of joy.
I find joy in others.
I find joy in my surroundings.
I am excited about my journey.
I create joy in my life.
My joy is limitless.
My joy is magnetic.
I am excited about my life.
I am excited about my opportunities.
I am excited about my purpose.
My soul is joyful.
I am full of joy.

Limitless

Opportunities are endless and limitless.
I decide what's possible for me.
I can do anything.
Everything is possible.
I am possible.
I can have everything I want.
My power is limitless.
I am redefining possibility.
I decide what's true for me.
I set my own limits.
I can do anything I say I can.
I am everything I want to be.
I am moving all obstacles in my life.
I am in control of my life.
I will conquer the world.
I am limitless.
My limits will never stop me.
I am breaking the chains over my life.
I see past the limitations.
The limits in my life are done.

Love

I am loveable.
I am loved.
I am worthy of receiving love.
I am loving.
I deserve love.
Many people love me.
I have loving relationships.
I love myself.
Love changes lives.
I know the power of love.
I share love with others.
Love is a gift.
I chose to love.
I make love a priority.
My love is unconditional.
My love is powerful.
Love is necessary.
I live in a place of love.
I have time for love.
I believe in love.

Money

I attract money with ease.
I am cash positive.
I am responsibility with money.
I can create and retain great amounts of wealth.
Money can change lives.
Money helps me help others.
Money is flowing in my life.
Money is necessary.
Money is a game changer.
I receive the blessing of money in my life.
I will give and receive money.
I am secure with my money.
I am aware of my money
Money brings new opportunities.
Money changes different situations.
My money works for me.
I have control over my money.
I am good with my spending.
I am educated about money.
I believe in my wealth.

Motivation

I am self-motivated.

I desire success.

I am willing to do what it takes.

I cultivate good habits.

I am motivated to be successful.

I have the mindset it takes to be successful.

I am determined to make it happen.

I am driven.

I will realize my goals.

I am motivated to make my dreams come true.

Motivation makes the dreams happen.

I see my dreams coming true.

I am making things happen.

I am moving towards greatness.

I am goal oriented.

My dreams are worth the work.

I have a circle of motivation.

I show others that things are possible.

I share my motivation.

I motivate others.

Patience

I am patient with others.
I am patient with my success.
Everything is working out when it is supposed to.
It's all good.
I am calm.
I am peaceful.
I will continue to act as long as it takes to realize my dreams.
I will keep going.
Things are working out for my good.
I know my greater is coming.
I can wait on my blessings.
My patience is a gift.
Patience is necessary.
Patience can change things.
I am believer in patience.
I know patience works.
Patience comes with love and kindness.
Success comes with patience.
I know my success is coming.
I am a patient person.

Peace

I am at peace.
I forgive others and I forgive myself.
I am calm.
I let go of my past mistakes.
I see the greatness in people.
I hold people in possibility.
We are all connected.
Peace is powerful.
I chose to be peaceful in my life.
Peace is powerful.
Peace surrounds me.
I create a peaceful environment.
Peace is a gift.
Peace changes lives.
Peace is necessary.
I chose to move on with my life.
I share peace with others.
I live in harmony with others.
I live in peace.
I am peaceful.

Power

I stand in my power.
I know I can do anything.
I am a powerful creator.
I can manifest miracles.
I have the power to do great things.
I am a powerful leader.
My power is limitless.
I have the power to create my future.
I have power to make my dreams come true.
I am powerful.
I can do great things.
I am a powerful person.
My power grows daily.
I am part of a power circle.
I live in a place of power.
I make power moves.
Power is necessary.
I live in my power.
I own my power.
I am a powerful force.

Prosperity

I am prosperous.
I have abundance in all areas of my life.
I have great relationships.
I have lots of money in the bank.
I have amazing health.
I make bucket-loads of money.
I can invest now.
I am cash positive.
I am financially free.
Making money is easy for me.
I am loving my life.
I am a money magnet.
I am growing my success.
I am growing my wealth.
I am debt free.
I will educate myself on money.
I will invest in myself.
I have a good relationship with money.
Money is good.
I love making money.

Relationships

People love me.
I have great friendships.
I have meaningful relationships.
I take time to cultivate relationships.
I value the people in my life closest to me.
I have loving relationships.
My family and friends are my greatest blessing.
I put my family and friends first.
My friends and family love me and understands me.
I take time to nurture my relationships.
I believe in my relationships.
My relationship grows daily.
My time to nurture my relationship is priceless.
My relationship has no conditions.
I am worthy of a real relationship.
I deserve true relationships.
I am part of a strong relationship.
Connections build relationships.
My relationships are powerful.
I have strong relationships.

Security

I am secure.
I am safe.
I am taken care of.
I place trust in abundance.
Everything will be okay.
I have financial security.
I have everything that I need.
God provides me everything that I require.
I am enough.
I am well.
All things are working out for my good.
I have a secure circle.
I feel safe with myself
I live in a secure environment.
My purpose is secure.
I am everything I need to be.
I am secure in my abilities.
I am secure in my life.
Secrets are safe with me.
I am in a safe place.

Self-Respect

I have self-respect
I believe in myself
My values are solid.
I will own my path.
I am enough.
I am my own cheerleader.
I respect myself.
I teach others how to treat me.
I live in authority.
I stand in my truth.
I respect myself.
I take time for me.
I honor myself.
I honor my values.
I honor God.
My body is the vessel of God.
I make healthy choices.
I respect my body.
I have a balanced life.
I value my integrity.

Self-Worth

I am perfect exactly as I am.
I deserve to follow my heart.
I deserve to take time for me.
I deserve to manifest miracles.
I am worthy.
I deserve to receive everything I have ever wanted.
I deserve to create wealth.
I am worthy of having valuable things.
I see my self worth.
I know that I am great.
I deserve the best things in life.
I live the life I want because I can.
I am ready for all life has to offer because it is my time.
I gain power from my self worth.
I feel my self worth grow daily.
I share the power of self worth with others.
I am destined for great things.
I know I am enough.
I go after my dreams because I deserve them.
I know I am worthy.

Strength

I am strong.
I am powerful.
I am motivated.
My faith is strong.
I have strong values.
I am a fighter.
I will fight for my dreams.
My strength has moved me to the next level.
I will make my life happen.
My power is real.
I live in my ideal body.
I have well defined muscles.
My body is rock solid.
People admire my strength.
I always persevere.
I am enough.
Every failure has made me stronger.
I have great inner strength.
God works through me.
My core is strong.

Success

I am committed to my success.
I am in control of my future.
I own my life.
I create my reality.
I am the CEO of my enterprise.
I attract money with ease.
I am successful in business.
I use my success to help others.
I grow success daily.
I own my success.
My success motivates others.
I help others be successful.
I am successful professionally and personally.
My success is limitless.
I live a life of my own design.
I make my dreams come true.
I am a successful person.
I move in the power of success.
I feel success flowing through me.
I am successful at all I do.

Trust

I trust in myself.
I trust in others.
I trust in the abundance of the universe.
I trust all things are working out for my good.
I trust there is a plan for my life.
I trust that I was born for a purpose.
I trust everything will be okay.
I trust in my ability to work things ok.
I trust in my ability to achieve my dreams.
I trust everything happens for a reason.
I am living in a place of trust.
I have a circle of trust.
There are many people I trust.
I know that people are trustworthy.
I am full of trust.
People recommend my skills.
I am moving in the right circles.
I am impacting lives.
People believe in me.
I am trustworthy.

Value

♥

I deserve to manifest miracles.
I deserve to receive everything I have ever wanted.
I deserve to create wealth.
I am worthy of having valuable things.
I am valuable.
I have value.
I see my value.
I see the value in others.
I have strong values.
I give value to everything I do.
I value the people in my life.
I am confident in my values.
My values make me who I am.
I feel the value growing in me.
I know that value is all around me.
I move in the direction of value.
My value grows every day.
I let others know they have value.
I share my values with others.
I live a life of value.

Victory

I will win.
I will succeed.
I am victorious.
I am more than a conqueror.
The battle is already won.
I am a victor.
I am a champion.
I am will see this through.
Victory is mine.
Everything will work out perfectly.
I will make it happen.
I live in my purpose.
I am on my way to greatness.
I am ready to shine.
I will prosper.
I live to win.
I am a survivor.
I am a game changer.
I am a winner.
I am an overcomer.

Vulnerability

It is okay to have flaws.
I have strength in weakness.
I am willing to be vulnerable.
I am perfect as I am.
I am complete just as I am.
I love all parts of myself.
I am free to be me.
I am strong enough to show my true selves to others.
People love me for who I am.
All parts of me are beautiful.
I am valuable.
I am me and I am enough.
I am in love with being me.
I value every part of me.
I am open to being all of me.
I live in being free.
I am ok letting my weakness show.
I am completely open.
I am ok with being me.
I let my feelings show.

Wealth

I attract money with easy.
I am great at creating wealth.
Money gives you the means to give more.
Money grows for me.
I have the skills to create wealth.
I am ready for wealth.
I am living a wealthy life.
I have wealth in all areas of my life.
I use my money wisely.
I give the money to charity.
I tithe to God.
I help others financially.
My finances are in order.
I am debt free.
I have money freedom.
I make strong financial decisions.
I live a life of giving.
I feel the money coming to me.
I think before I spend.
I will manage my money well.

Wisdom

I am wise.
I exercise good judgment.
People seek my advice and counsel.
I make good decisions.
I make wise choices.
People respect my opinions.
I am connected to the wisdom of the universe.
I am in touch with my higher consciousness.
Everything I need to know is revealed to me.
I already know the answer.
I surround myself with wise people.
I constantly grow in wisdom.
I am an expert in my field.
I develop my skills and wisdom.
I live to learn.
I am a life long learning.
I crave wisdom daily.
I find wisdom valuable.
I love wisdom.
My decisions are rooted in wisdom.